Dance with Desire

Irving Layton ∿
Dance With Desire
SELECTED LOVE POEMS

Drawings by Richard Gorman

The Porcupine's Quill

NATIONAL LIBRARY OF CANADA
CATALOGUING IN PUBLICATION DATA

Layton, Irving, 1912–
  Dance with desire

Poems.
ISBN 0-88984-135-7

I. Gorman, Richard, 1935– . II. Lake Galleries. III. Title.

PS8523.A87D3 1992 C811'.54 C92-093769-1
PR9199.3.L38D3 1992

3 4 5 • 04 03 02

Published by The Porcupine's Quill
68 Main Street, Erin, Ontario NOB 1TO
www.sentex.net / ˜pql

Readied for the press by John Metcalf. The cover and incidental
drawings are by Richard Gorman. Typeset in Ehrhardt, printed on
Zephyr Antique laid, and bound at the Porcupine's Quill Inc.

Represented in Canada by the Literary Press Group.
Trade orders are available from General Distribution Services.

We acknowledge the support of the Ontario Arts Council,
and the Canada Council for the Arts for our publishing program.
The financial support of the Government of Canada through the Book
Publishing Industry Development Program is also gratefully
acknowledged.

Canadä

For Miss Benjamin – the Grade Six teacher
who awakened my erotic impulses
and inspired my first sensual poem.

Foreword ∽

William Wordsworth was turned on by daffodils; I'm turned on by
women. He saw their golden cups tossing beside the lake and
stored the sight away in his mind to give him a lift whenever he
felt vacant or depressed. I treasure the sight of firm-titted women
walking on Avenue Road or St. Catherine Street. He didn't pluck
every daffodil he celebrated, nor have I every woman I've written
poems for and now lay gratefully between the covers of this book.

My first poem was to a Grade Six teacher, Miss Benjamin. I
yearned for her as only a horny pre-adolescent can who doesn't
know what to do with his impulses, a riot of romanticism, idealism
and burgeoning sensuality. I can still recall the excitement 'in the
blood' I felt each time she entered the classroom, the dizziness and
rapture I experienced when I looked up and saw her dimples, the
lovely flush of her cheeks, her wavy brown hair. I used to pretend I
had some difficulty with the arithmetic problem she had set the
class to get her to bend over my desk so that I might see the
crimson tinge that began at her chin and went right down to her
tantalizing cleavage. Indeed, it has often occurred to me that every
woman I've ever loved has been a materialization of Miss
Benjamin, the fleshly incarnation of my boyhood desire for her.

Everything poets write about when they describe the delirium
and ecstasy of love I have known from that time on. It has been
difficult, sometimes impossible to give my attention to anything
else; difficult for my mind with its penchant for abstractions and
concepts to trick my heart into paying them the slightest heed or
consideration. How can anyone who has known the intensities of
love, its sudden spirallings upward to glory or downward to
disaster and grief seriously entertain for any length of time notions
on politics, religion, philosophy, literature, or even the meaner
appetites and ambitions prevalent upon this planet. 'The food of
love' is the only kind I've ever cared to eat, the only food I've ever
hungered for. And talking about food: didn't I bolt down tiny black
pellets of goat dung because I didn't want my first love, watching
me pick them up in her backyard, to think that her eleven-year-old

gallant couldn't tell the difference between them and olives? Symbol or omen? Foretaste of things to come? Metaphor for the inescapable paradoxes of love? All these, of course.

I may have written two- or three-hundred love poems since my first one for Miss Benjamin. Many of them with more propriety could be called hate poems, for surely love and hate are two sides of the coin we call sexual interest or desire. For the present collection I've tried to cull those poems that when put together in one volume will give the reader the startling thrill of a *déjà vu*. I want him to exclaim with understanding, amusement and sympathy: 'Yes, the writer of these verses knows what he's talking about. He has really been there, on those scarred slopes inhabited by "La Belle Dame Sans Merci". He has paid for them in agony and exaltation for they have the authentic feel only personal knowledge can confer, without which poems are as lifeless as a pickled fetus. Only someone who has been on those slopes can have reproduced so faithfully the glory and carnage of the love emotion.'

What is the love emotion? When you are lost and most yourself. Or to be comical and light-hearted about the matter: when you are a Sufi with Sophie on the sofa and you feel most alive, most intensely yourself and most generous.

When the antinomies of existence dissolve and dance into one another, merging into a music one hears at no other time; when clapping your hands with them as they melt into oneness you behold in a moment of ecstatic vision the seamless unity of creation. At that moment dictator and tyrant are worms' food and you know with luminous certainty that all who hanker after titles and money are sick unhappy cripples the world would do beautifully without.

Let the philosophers rave on about the *summum bonum* and mystics about embracing God. They are still vertical humans and therefore even their adorations still have something aggressive about them. Humans in the horizontal position have always struck me as less likely to be violent and destructive. So I take my place beside the poets, and less arrogant than the philosopher or mystic, am prepared to find the greatest good and embrace God whenever I hold a woman in the act of love. It is then I know with assurance and inexpressible delight that whatever it is life promises us, this must be it; and that a universe containing this experience must have something grandly important going for it. That is, finally, when all the subtractions are made, what the love poems in this book are all about.

Irving Layton

'They dance best who dance with desire.'
– *A Red Carpet for the Sun*

To the Girls of My Graduating Class

Wanting for their young limbs praise,
Their thighs, hips, and saintly breasts,
They grow from awkwardness to delight,
Their mouths made perfect with the air
About them and the sweet rage in the blood,
The delicate trouble in their veins.

Intolerant as happiness, suddenly
They'll dart like bewildered birds;
For there's no mercy in that bugler Time
That excites against their virginity
The massed infantry of days, nor in the tendrils
Greening on their enchanted battlements.

Golda, Fruma, Dinnie, Elinor,
My saintly wantons, passionate nuns;
O light-footed daughters, your unopened
Brittle beauty troubles an aging man
Who hobbles after you a little way
Fierce and ridiculous.

1953

How Poems Get Written

Like
a memory
torn
at the shoulder,
my darling
wears
the chemise
I gave her –
a wedding gift.

At night
I tap out
my poems
on her hip bone.

When
she can't
sleep
either,
we write
the poem
together.

1954

Portrait of Aileen

Unlike others, near cousins to fatuity,
you walked carelessly into my thoughts of you;
and with a tired movement of your eyelids
defined yourself to me
under your absurd hair.

To begin with, I had never seen
so much sadness on a woman's mouth.
There were no answers for your grief.
My curiosity like a trained domestic
left everything as before, as if untouched.

Though an incredible wound in the air
the bowl of apples on the garden table
sustained itself with simply being.
It is the architecture of sanity, I thought.
But you wove the air with charred fingers.

'The centrality of the fly,' you said,
'it's impassive, a black demi-god. The
flowers choke the weeds. No matter.'
The look on your face appalled at being there
has taught me severity, exactness of speech.

1954

Marie

Believes men want one thing only
                 And she's got it
High or low, learned or ignorant,
– To pluck the dark rose below her navel

She thinks also
That I'm a poor lover: I
Am too romantick
                 She herself is not so

She uses sentiment like a perfume:
To stimulate action
                 She is always ready

She says when she closes her eyes
She can see men's hands waving plantlike
Under the table, undulating towards her dress:
Her thighs: her IT
                 their lips moving
As if they were playing harmonicas
In a harmonica band
Lips: teeth, lips: teeth, words, words, words
        But she never attends to the words

She likes to feel that their pale hands
Are out there seeking her panties
And when I ask her what she's thinking of
She invariably answers:
>   O, certain childhood memories

Tell that to Tennyson and to Ezra
Of the troubadours

1954

Misunderstanding

I placed
my hand
upon
her thigh.

By the way
she moved
away
I could see
her devotion
to literature
was not
perfect.

1954

For Louise, Age 17

She came to us recommended
By the golden minutes and by nothing else;
Her skin glowed, sang with the compliments
Which these same minutes paid her.

Her hair burned like a yellow fire
To celebrate the strange beauty of her face;
Herself, she walked unconscious
Of the need she started in us to praise, admire

The elegance we found in us
Like a vein of rare silver when we saw her;
But all our thoughts were caught in the compass
Of her royal arms and we sank down

Into the dark where the blood sings after dark,
Into the light because it was the light,
Into the clear valley where her body was made,
Her beauty had lain, now resurrected

Raised by the minutes which start, slay,
Their ivory hafts fiery with sun-motes
Which, crying, we seized to make an immortal ring
For beauty which is its own excuse and never dies.

1955

I Would for Your Sake Be Gentle

I would for your sake be gentle
Be, believe me, other than I am:
What, what madness is it that hurls me
Sundays against your Sunday calm?

True, there's enough gall in my ducts
To cover an area, and more:
But why you – free from evil, poor bird?
Why you – my heart and saviour?

I swear I'm damned to so hate and rage.
But your fair innocence is my guilt;
And the stream that you make clear
I must, to fog my image, fill with silt.

Bear with me, bear with me –
Your goodness, gift so little understood
Even by the angels I suppose
And by us here somewhat undervalued

Is what I hold to when madness comes.
It is the soft night against which I flare
Rocketwise, and when I fall
See my way back by my own embers.

1955

La Minerve

And if I say my dog's vivid tongue
Clapped the frogs under their green fables,
Or the rock's coolness under my hand
Told me clearly which way the sun passed

And if I say in a clean forest
I heard myself proclaimed a traitor
By the excellent cones, for I thought
Where the good go, green as an apple

And if like our French grocer, Mailloux,
I lay these things on your white table
With a hot involuntary look,
And add a word about the first gods

I take satisfaction from your smile
And the inclination of your shoulder
Before the birds leave off their singing
And slowly the dark fills up my eyes

But when you stand at night before me
Like the genius of this place, naked,
All my ribs most unpaganlike ache
With foolstruck Adam in his first wonder.

1955

Orpheus

Poets of a distant time
Mix madness with your rhyme
And with my dust I'll weave
    Dark rhymes for your reprieve

God was not Love nor Law,
God was the blood I saw,
The ever-flowing blood
    Staining water and sod

Woman I loved. Enough
She made me dream of love
And in that sexual dream
    Forget the whitethroat's scream

Saw men could finer sing
For someone's suffering
Laugh with you and after
    Envy you for your laughter

O these talented beasts
Might on your dead eyes feast,
Or pluck them from your head
    Plant jonquils in their stead

And with your dying spasm
Sing loose their gates of prison
Yet this transforming song
       Engender bitter wrong

Saw they could demolish
With love love's foliage
And that the poet's heart
       Has nowhere counterpart

Which can celebrate
Love equally with Death
Yet by its pulsing bring
       A music into everything

1955

Love's Diffidence

Love is so diffident a thing.
I scoop up my hands with air;
I do not find it there
Nor in my friend's pleasure
Nor when the birds sing.

I am confused, forsaken.
I have lost the way.
Love's not as some men say
In woman's eyes, blue or grey;
Nor in kisses given and taken.

Love, I call out, find me
Spinning round in error.
Display your dank, coarse hair,
Your bubs and bulbous shoulder.
Then strike, witless bitch, blind me.

1955

By Ecstasies Perplexed

By that, by this, by sharp ecstasies perplexed,
illumined, a saint streaked with foibles,
    I wore at the heart a hairshirt of fire,
wrapped my thighs in a loincloth of bees.

Honour forswore and talent, and with these
burnished those blue-dyed baubles which hang
    amorously from sad and arid bantam trees
in one-room apartments cheaply furnished.

Yet now with lust and indignation spent
and even remorse and other troubles
    I ask whether by deliberate will I went
or frenzy at a woman's beauty.

And cannot answer. But recall
a flaxen-haired boy five years old
    who one bad night put fire to his gown
and watched the flames about him rise blue and gold.

1956

Thanatos and Eros

One night beside her spouse suddenly
Her heart was ambushed and her naked
Buttocks quivered with death's agony;
Her shoulders twitched, she gave a low cry.
Love's frolic the weak churl thought and shed
Hot seed against her indifferent thigh.

1956

Obit

The hour when I lose life
My friend made ill by grief
At once takes to his bed
With my poor darling Kit;
Laments in her white arms
My cold expired limbs,
And since her naked flesh
Such perfect marble is
Erects betwixt her and him
A towering headstone.

Alas, his mind is grief-crazed
(Interment all its image)
And into her roomy crypt
His rude memorial
With no delay he slips
While kissings ring its knell.
More! Writes on her mound of tit
A friend's flowing tribute
Spurred on by her frequent sighs
And praise of his fine merit:
Till he too all distracted
Groans and with a shudder dies!

1956

Nausicäa

'I'm the sort of girl
      you must first tell you love.'
'I love you,' I said.
She gave herself to me then
  and I enjoyed her on her perfumed bed.

By the gods, the pleasure in her small
      wriggling body was so great,
  I had spoken no lecherous falsehood.
Now not I nor my beloved,
      such is our heat,
can wait for either words or scented sheet
but on her or my raincoat go roughly to it.

1956

Woman

Vain and not to trust
unstable as wind,
as the wind ignorant;
shallow, her laugh
jarring my mended teeth.
I spit out
the loose silver
from my aching mouth.

With candid gaze
she meets my jealous
look, and is false.
Yet I am lost, lost.
Beauty and pleasure,
fatal gifts,
she brings in her thighs,
in her small amorous body.

O not remembering
her derision of me,
I plunge like a corkscrew
into her softness,
her small wicked body
and there, beyond reproach,
I roar like a sick lion
between her breasts.

1956

Undine

Your body to hold, your perfect breasts.
Your lips; your hips under my pregnant hands
        That when they move, why, they're snakes
Sliding, and hiding near your golden buttocks.

Then as your great engines of love begin
Intestinal, furious, submarine
        They spark into small bites
Whose hot spittle inundates all my deserts.

And I'm like water in a scoop of stone
Kissed into absence by a drying sun;
        Or I'm dried Sahara sand
Wanting your wetness over me without end.

So possessed, so broken's my entire self
No rosy whipcord, love, can bind my halves
        When queen you squat; you moisten
My parched nipples into a blazing garden.

And I your paramour-Paracelsus
Fish a soul for you from between my loins;
        You shudder in my embrace
And all your wetness takes the form of tears.

1956

Bargain

In fourteen years
        of married bliss
not once have I been disloyal
to my wife;
and you, I am told, are still
a virgin.

If you are set
        to barter your maidenhead
for my unheard-of fidelity,
call me between three and five tomorrow
and it is done.

1956

Song for a Late Hour

No one told me
to beware your bracelets,
the winds I could expect
from your small breasts.
No one told me
the tumult of your hair.
When a lock touched me
I knew the sensations
of shattering glass.

Your kissings put
blue water around me.
I would look at you
with bold Cretan mirth:
I would forget
I am a cringing semite,
a spaniel suffering
about your tight skirts.

I slabber for your rippling
hips, your white shoulders.
I am sick
with love of you. Girl, O girl,
let our washed limbs make
a perverse Star of David
and cones of flesh,
Cythera all night
at my silvered back.

1956

Letter from a Straw Man

I loved you, Bobbo, even when you knuckled me
And pulled the straw out of my breast,
Pretending to weep yet secretly glad to note
How yellow and summer-dry the stuff was.

You will surely recall how amazed
We both were the straw was endless;
At the time I did not know it was your fingers
Made the straw grow there and blaze

Yellow in the fierce sunlight.... How when
I once caught your cold blue eye
It first burned like sulphur, but affected
Let down a tear like a drop of dirty sea-water

Into my prized-open chest; though after
That encounter of our eyes, your own –
The pitiful one – grew into a porcelain saucer
White and blind. That I could understand.

But why did you give great handfuls
To the visiting firemen? And when the mayor
Asked for some to decorate his fireplace,
Why did you not refuse? No, rather,

Plunging your green delicate fingers
Into my gaping breast you drew
Out for him the longest stalk
Which he snatched with a cough and a compelling eye.

I have left you for another,
Who wears black panties and is as crazy as the birds;
But when the straw comes away in her hands
She is careful to burn it immediately afterwards.

1956

Holiday

'Quebec roads are damned tricky,' he shouted
To his wife out on the lake rowing;
'Adrien's girl will travel a-ways with me,
But I do not know why or where she's going.'

He saw his stolid wife drop from the boat
And stand, the water around her flowing;
And he saw the bent father near the shore
Where the farm tumbled into weed, mowing.

The sensual sun was mounted on a hill.
His passion too was mounting, O growing
With each quick step in unison they took;
And where the road dipped, he felt like crowing.

Black horse dung, stones, and yellow butterflies;
A young bull and his herd of cows lowing;
The white cock fastened on top the roadside cross
That could not tell which way the wind was blowing.

1956

Rain

The wind blew hard in the trees
And palegreen was the wet grass;
I love you, Love, my Sweet said
And gave her false mouth to kiss.

Huge leopard spots the rain put
On the stone near where we sat;
An obscure song at our feet
Sang the troubled rivulet.

In front the black road went by,
A panther in search of prey;
Between some mouldering firs
I lay down her bleeding corse.

The wind blew hard in the trees
And screeched in the low briars;
I loved you truly, I said
And kissed her false dead mouth.

The rain fell, decaying eyes
And small ears; how green the moss!
Let her red lips kiss the rot
In their last quiver of death.

The white rain shall knit her shroud
And clean my hands of her blood;
The cottage on the round lake
Blind that eye like a cataract.

1958

Sacrament by the Water

How shall I sing the accomplished waters
Whose teeming cells make green my hopes
How shall the Sun at daybreak marry us
Twirling these waters like a hoop.

Gift of the waters that sing
Their eternal passion for the sky,
Your perfect beauty in a wave of tumult
Drops an Eden about your thighs.

Green is the singing water
And green is every joyous leaf
White myrtle's in your hand and in the other
The hairy apple bringing life.

1959

Berry Picking

Silently my wife walks on the still wet furze
Now darkgreen the leaves are full of metaphors
Now lit up is each tiny lamp of blueberry.
The white nails of rain have dropped and the sun is free.

And whether she bends or straightens to each bush
To find the children's laughter among the leaves
Her quiet hands seem to make the quiet summer hush –
Berries or children, patient she is with these.

I only vex and perplex her; madness, rage
Are endearing perhaps put down upon the page;
Even silence daylong and sullen can then
Enamour as restraint or classic discipline.

So I envy the berries she puts in her mouth,
The red and succulent juice that stains her lips;
I shall never taste that good to her, nor will they
Displease her with a thousand barbarous jests.

How they lie easily for her hand to take,
Part of the unoffending world that is hers;
Here beyond complexity she stands and stares
And leans her marvellous head as if for answers.

No more the easy soul my childish craft deceives
Nor the simpler one for whom yes is always yes;
No, now her voice comes to me from a far way off
Though her lips are redder than the raspberries.

1959

The Day Aviva Came to Paris

The day you came naked to Paris
The tourists returned home without their guidebooks,
The hunger in their cameras finally appeased.

Alone once more with their gargoyles, the Frenchmen
Marvelled at the imagination that had produced them
And once again invited terror into their *apéritifs*.
Death was no longer exiled to the cemeteries.

In their royal gardens where the fish die of old age,
They perused something else besides newspapers
– A volume perhaps by one of their famous writers.
They opened their hearts to let your tender smile defrost them;
Their livers filled with an unassuageable love of justice.
They became the atmosphere around them.

They learned to take money from Americans
Without a feeling of revulsion towards them;
And to think of themselves
As not excessively subtle or witty.
'*Au diable* with Voltaire,' they muttered,
'Who was a national calamity.
Au diable with *la République*.'
(A race of incurable *petits bourgeois*, the French
Are happiest under a horse under a man)
'*Au diable* with *la Monarchie!*
We saw no goddesses during either folly;
Our bald-headed savants never told us
Such a blaze of pubic hair anywhere existed.'
And they ordered the grandson of Grandma Moses
To paint it large on the dome of le Sacré-Coeur.

My little one, as if under those painted skies
It was again 1848,
They leaped as one mad colossal Frenchman from their café Pernods
Shouting, *'Vive l'Australienne!*
Vive Layton who brought her among us!
Let us erect monuments of black porphyry to them!
Let us bury them in the Panthéon!'
(*Pas si vite, messieurs;* we are still alive)

And when, an undraped Jewish Venus,
You pointed to a child, a whole slum starving in her eyes,
Within earshot of the Tuileries,
The French who are crazy or catholic enough
To place, facing each other, two tableaux
– One for the Men of the Convention, and one puffing the
            Orators of the Restoration –
At once made a circle wide as the sky around you
While the Mayor of the 5th Arrondissement
Addressed the milling millions of Frenchmen:

'See how shapely small her adorable ass is;
Of what an incredible pink rotundity each cheek.
A bas Merovingian and Valois!
A bas Charlemagne and Henri Quatre!
For all the adulations we have paid them
In our fabulous *histoires*
They cannot raise an erection between them. Ah,
For too long has the madness of love
Been explained to us by sensualists and *curés.*
A bas Stendhal! *A bas* Bossuet!

'Forever and forever, from this blazing hour
All Paris radiates from Aviva's nest of hair
– Delicate hatchery of profound delights –

From her ever-to-be-adored Arche de Triomphe!
All the languors of history
Take on meaning clear as a wineglass or the belch of an angel
Only if thought of as rushing
On the wings of a rhinoceros towards this absorbing event.
Voyeurs, voyez! The moisture of her delicate instep
Is a pool of love
Into which sheathed in candy paper
Anaesthetized politicians drop from the skies!'
(Word jugglery of course, my Sweet; but the French love it
– Mistake it in fact for poetry)

And the *applaudissements* and bravos
Bombinating along the boulevard Saint-Germain
Made the poor docile Seine
Think our great Atlantic was upon it.
It overflowed with fright into the bookstalls
And sidewalk cafés.
Fifteen remaining *allemands* with their cameras
Were flushed down the rue Pigalle.

And when you were raised up
Into my hairy arms by the raving emotional crowds
Waving frenzied bottles of Beaujolais
And throwing the corks away ecstatically
(Not saving them!)
It was, my Love, my Darling,
As if someone had again ordered an advance
Upon the Bastille
Which we recalled joyously, face to face at last,
Yielded after only a small token resistance.

1961

Dans le Jardin

Dearest girl, my hands are too fond of flesh
For me to speak to you; and you are too tall
For me to think you beautiful, though beautiful
You are. You are some other's fortunate wish

Though alone and your idle limbs inviting.
If I should call to you, give you this verse
And later caress your thighs with these fingers
You would rise like a wraith, like some wan Viking

Come from the North, mists upon her shoulders.
Your eyes are too grave and too luminous
And pledge but one cold nocturnal kiss,
Their gaze putting out the fires that it stirs

Till I hear bells, a slowly dying sound,
Where no bells are; how then should I suppose
You passionately flinging off skirt and blouse
And letting my squat body pin you to the ground?

So as you move your blanket and thin buttocks
To catch the failing sunlight on your face,
I watch you from my stationary place,
My limbs as immovable as these planted rocks

And think of Fate and of your immoderate height
And of your spoiling gauntness; and of what blind
Excuse to make the ceremonious stars who'll find
Our bodies uncoupled by the coming night.

1961

The Convertible

Her breath already smelled of whisky.
She lit a cigarette
And pointed to a flask in the glove compartment.
Then our mouths met.

She placed her hand on my groin;
She hadn't bothered to remove her wedding ring.
Her eyes closed with a sigh.
I was ready for the gathering.

You, Dulla, may prefer maidenheads;
But give me the bored young wives of Hampstead
Whose husbands provide them with smart convertibles
And who are reasonably well-read.

1961

Androgyne

Were Death a woman I should never die.
So jealous is my loving wife that I
Could look upon a passing hearse and sneer
At this dumb show of frail mortality.
For what from Death would I have then to fear

Who might not even by her darkest guile,
Her frowned commands, her most sensual smile,
Tear me from my Love? Tell me, who'd encroach
On her whose fingers stiffen to a file,
Seeing a woman from afar approach?

No, certainly I shall live forever;
For my dear wife will be immortal too
As one whom Death, androgynous lover,
Rages against my jealousy to woo.
Only by dread compact shall we be free
For waiting Death to ravish her and me.

1963

Elegy for Marilyn Monroe

Last summer, it was 'Papa' Hemingway,
This summer, it's Marilyn Monroe.
Next summer, who? – Who will it be?
But Orville Faubus gets re-elected
Two hundred million Ex-Laxed Americans
    go on defecating as before
and Congress acts as if nothing has happened.

How come I asked of Lyndon Johnson
    there's no committee
to investigate
the high rate of suicide
among those with a tragic overplus
of sensitivity and consciousness;
and received a postcard
    showing a Texas oil field.

Gentlemen, take it for what it's worth
but I suspect something more terrible
    than radioactive fallout
or the unmentionable gases of Belsen
has penetrated our human atmosphere.
The PTA's haven't heard of it yet
or the Board of Directors of Bell Tel
or President Kennedy;
moreover if I manoeuvred to let them know
    what it is
there'd be a Congressional committee
to investigate me!
They'd get cracking at once. O yes.

You ask, what is it
that goes straight for its victims like radar?
I name it the Zed-factor,

lethal only to the passionate, the imaginative,
    and to whatever is rare and delightful
in this brute universe.
Invisible as halitosis or body odour
it makes no warning of its presence;
therefore no TV outfit
will sing commercials to it
with chuckling hooligans
    poking fingers through plugged drains,
and anyhow since only an infinitesimal part
of the nation
is susceptible to attack
why bother? See, why bother?

Goodbye Marilyn
It's raining in Magog
    a town you probably never heard of
where I sit in a tavern writing this;
nor did you ever hear of me
though I once composed a whole poem to you
and called you 'Earth Goddess'.
The janitors to whom you said hello,
the cabbies who spotted you by your stride
    and magnificent blonde hair
and whistled and honked their horns
to let you know their good luck,
the men all around the world
who touched your limbs in irreverent sleep
will miss your wiggle and crazy laugh,
but no one more than I
dazed this afternoon by grief and drink;
for I loved you from the first
who know what they do not know,

seeing in your death a tragic portent
for all of us who crawl and die
under the wheeling, disappearing stars;
and who must now live with the self-complacent,
    the enduring dull,
without your sustaining radiance,
your rarity.

From here on in
they have it, the pygmies have it,
it's all theirs!

Goodbye Marilyn
Sleep, sleep peacefully tonight
One poet at least will remember
    your brightness,
the unique fever in your form and face
(O insuperable filament, now black, now ash!)
and love you always.

1963

The Bishopric

Yes, and finding my small friar
sullen, cowled and scowling
in his beggar's posture:

Ha, my voice went sour
for the college girl squirming
under my length of form.
'I must reread my own poems,'
I said bitterly. 'Or so it seems.'

'Luckily for you,' she breathed,
'no one will ever believe this
– not even your worst biographer.'

I roared and that did it.
There was an instant election
as she brought her youthful face,
laughing,
into the sweet diocese of my body.

1963

The Well-Wrought Urn

'What would you do
if I suddenly died?'

'Write a poem to you.'

'Would you mourn for me?'

'Certainly,' I sighed.

'For a long time?'

'That depends.'

'On what?'

'The poem's excellence,' I replied.

1963

For Aviva, Because I Love Her

I saw a spider eating a huge bee.

First he ate my limbs;
and then he removed my head, feasting
  on the quivering jellies of my eyes
and on what passes among bees for ears.

And though dead,
I could feel, with each morsel he had,
that he enjoyed his repast
  and I was glad.

Afterwards he sliced me down the middle,
exposing my insides
  to the burning mid-day heat;
and slowly the voluptuous spider
feasted on my jewelled organs,
abolishing them one by one,
till I was all gone, all swallowed up,
  except for my love of you:

My radiant wings – these, ah, these
he did not touch
but left glinting in the sun.

1963

Bicycle Pump

The idle gods for laughs gave man his rump;
In sport, so made his kind that when he sighs
In ecstasy between a woman's thighs
He goes up and down, a bicycle pump;
And his beloved once his seed is sown
Swells like a faulty tube on one side blown.

1964

For My Green Old Age

Your eyes, lips, voice:
these I could withstand;
but when you unbuttoned your blouse
to show me the pink shapeliness
                              of your breasts,
my fingers like five sentinels
trembled with surprise;
warts and all my wisdom I sang away
and the cigarette's irresolute ash
splashed on my stiff trouser leg like water.

Was it a beautiful woman's malice
or her mockery
made you turn and say,
standing there like Eve's naked daughter:
        'Since you cannot find the ashtray,
how will you what's between my thighs?'

Whatever, and who cares:
when I am a greyhead full of years
I shall tell the priests and rabbis
about your gaiety
and of how to keep my hand from trembling
you pressed it between your thighs.

1964

The Seduction

First he knocks her down
   by assaulting her soul;
telling her she's vain, superficial,
and adding – to drive his point home –
   that she's frivolous
and terribly, terribly selfish.

She takes the bait
   like the blonde fish she is
and for whole weeks goes about
beating her lovely breasts
   till her niplets
look like congealed drops of blood.
O she's full of remorse,
   full of remorse for all
her past egocentric, thoughtless ways,
and she sighs and cries a great deal.

Remorse in women
   is a sure-fire aphrodisiac:
they can't bear to be thought less than perfect
and so their contribution
is actually a variant form of vanity
and vanity is a great quickener
   of the sexual appetite.
Everything about them, in fact, is false
except passion; only in their desire
for intercourse are they completely sincere.

This with a priest's cunning my rival knew
   as well as I myself now do:
Judging her sufficiently broken,
   humbled and contrite,

~

he thinks the moment exactly right
   to toss her some small compliment
as one tosses a bone to a famished bitch.
(He praised, I think, her fidelity to friends.)
The colour swoops back into her cheeks,
her eyes put on their fetching impertinence,
for the first time in weeks she laughs.

She's grateful,
   and when a woman is grateful
she has many ways of expressing her sense
of the occasion
but naturally prefers the easiest
   and most pleasant one.
In this, my Lucy was no exception.
Her gratitude is immense,
yet no greater than the provocation had been
which now stretches her out
   in perfect humility
while he rises beautifully to the occasion.
He dazes her with sweet, forgiving kisses
and all the long and lazy afternoon
   they're mutual as thieves in a cell
and, ah, tender as they come.

1964

Creation

I fashioned you:
Composed you between darkness and dawn.

You are my best-made poem,
The one I laboured longest over.

What does one do with a poem?
One gives it to the world.

Go, darling, delight others
As you have delighted me.

Bring your fragrant freshness
To lover and lover.

In their loins sow madness and fever
That my fame may endure forever.

1964

With the Money I Spend

With the money I spend on you
I could buy ice cream for Korean kings.
I could adopt a beggar
    and clothe him in scarlet and gold.
I could leave a legacy of dolls and roses
        to my grandchildren.
Why must you order expensive Turkish cigarettes?
And why do you drink only the most costly champagne?
The Leninists are marching on us.
Their eyes are inflamed with social justice.
Their mouths are contorted with the brotherhood of man.
Their fists are heavy with universal love.
They have not read a line of Mayakovsky's poems
    for twelve whole months.
The deprivation has made them desperate.
With staring eyeballs they hold off
    waiting for the ash from your cigarette to fall.
That is the signal.
When the ash crumbles, the man with the smallest forehead
    will smash a cracked hourglass, the sound
        amplified into a thousand manifestos.
Can you not see them? Can you not hear them?
Already they are closing in on us.
Your fragrant body means nothing to them.
Under your very eyes, velvet and remarkable,
    they intone that Beauty is not absolute.
They shout for an unobstructed view of your shoulders,
    your proud and beautiful head gone.
They will break your arms and slender legs
    into firewood.
The golden delicate hairs I have kissed
    into fire a thousand times
        will blaze more brightly;
But who will bend down to gather the flames

into their mouth?
Who will follow their white light into eternity?

Because I love you better
    than artichokes and candles in the dark,
I shall speak to them.
Perhaps they will overlook your grace for my sake,
    ignore the offending perfection of your lips.
Perhaps, after all, you and I will start
    a mass conversion into elegance.
I will tell them my father made cheese
    and was humble and poor all his life,
And that his father before him turned ill
    at the mere sight of money;
And that a certain remote ancestor of mine
    never saw money at all,
        having been born blind.
On my mother's side, they were all failures.
Calliopes will sound for my undistinguished lineage
And the aroused Leninists will at once guess
    I am a fool in love, a simpleton,
        an ensnared and deranged proletarian
With no prospects but the wind which exposes
    my terrible hungers to them,
My counter-revolutionary appetite to be lost
    from all useful labour
        in your arms hair thighs navel;
And parting the clouds, one solitary star
    to show them where I am slain
Counting the gold coins
    for your Turkish cigarettes and costly champagne.

1965

For Musia's Grandchildren

I write this poem
for your grandchildren
for they will know of your loveliness
only from hearsay,
from yellowing photographs
spread out on table and sofa
for a laugh.

When arrogant
with the lovely grace you gave their flesh
they regard your dear frail body pityingly,
your time-dishonoured cheeks
pallid and sunken
and those hands
that I have kissed a thousand times
mottled by age
and stroking a grey ringlet into place,
I want them suddenly
to see you as I saw you
– beautiful as the first bird at dawn.

Dearest love, tell them
that I, a crazed poet all his days
who made woman
his ceaseless study and delight,
begged but one boon
in this world of mournful beasts
that are almost human:
to live praising your marvellous eyes
mischief could make glisten
like winter pools at night
or appetite put a fine finish on.

1967

A Song About Woman

I put all that I knew
    about woman
into a pearl-lined shell
and flung it into the sea;
but a wave rose up like a fist
    and seized it
and hurled it back at me.
The waves stood up like a chorus
    and I heard them hiss:
'We have monsters enough in our deeps
without this.'

I put all that I knew
    about woman
into an air-tight box
and shot it into the sky;
but someone behind a cloud
    put out a hand and flung it
back to the sand and rocks;
while a cloud muffled his words
and the sky hung like a shroud
    his words came down as rain
and the rain was thick as curds.

I put all that I knew
    about woman
into a jewelled urn
and buried it in the ground;
but at once the grasses parted
    and flowers began to turn
and the thing that I had buried
    came up without a sound.
'Fool,' said a voice full of mirth
'she is perfect, my lovely daughter!'
Then still were the lips of earth.

1967

To a Beautiful Unknown Girl

All morning I struggled to write a poem

I thought of my childhood
that had rolled like a button under the bed
and was lost forever

Of the armless virtuoso
who lit my wife's flaming cherry jubilee
with his nimble toes

Of my mother dying in the hospital

Of girls walking towards
all the beaches of the world
with NO PARKING printed on their rear ends

Of God finally unmasking himself
in a public square like Zorro

Of pebbles that sang arias
from my favourite operas
whenever I dropped them into the sea

Of love which I had forgotten to take out
from the drawer where I keep my neckties

But when the beautiful unknown girl
came towards me
holding the French poodle in her long graceful arms

I threw away my imperfect lines
what was the use?
She was the poem I had wanted to write

1967

An Old Niçoise Whore

The famous and rich, even the learned and wise,
    Singly or in pairs went to her dwelling
To press their civilized lips to her thighs
    Or learn at first hand her buttocks' swelling.

Of high-paying customers she had no lack
    And was herself now rich: so she implied.
Mostly she had made her pile while on her back
    But sometimes she had made it on the side.

Reich she read; of course the Viennese doctor.
    Lawrence – his poems and novels she devoured;
Kafka at the beginning almost rocked her
    But as she read him more she said he soured.

Swedish she spoke, French, Polish, fluent German;
    Had even picked up Hindi – who knows how?
In bed she had learned to moan and sigh in Russian
    Though its rhythms troubled her even now.

A nymphomaniac like Napoleon's sister
    She could exhaust a bull or stallion;
Bankers had kneeled before her crotch to kiss her
    And ex-princes, Spanish and Italian.

And all the amorous mayors of France-Sud
    Impelled by lust or by regional pride
Would drive their Renaults into her neighbourhood,
    Ring her bell and troop happily inside.

And pimpled teenagers whom priests and rabbis
    Had made gauche, fearful, prurient and blind
Prodded by Venus had sought her expert thighs:
    Ah, to these she was especially kind.

And having translated several Swinburne lines
    She kept the finest whips she could afford
To be (though most aristocrats brought their canes)
    Ready for some forgetful English lord.

We saw waves like athletes dash towards the shore
    Breaking it seemed from a line of green scum;
We saw the sun dying, and this aged whore
    Noted how it gave clouds a tinge of rum.

Engaging was her mien, her voice low and sweet;
    Convent nuns might have envied her address.
She was touched by the bathers below her feet;
    I, by this vitality sprung from cess.

And as she spoke to me on the crowded quay
    And reminisced about her well-spent years
I mourned with her her shrivelled face and body
    And gave what no man had given her: tears.

1967

Apparition

Thinking of you, I could not sleep

You came into the tenebrous room
like moonlight
and sat on the chair like a pool of light

I was too awed to touch you

I waited for you to speak
There was a sudden flicker
(of amusement? distress?)
and then you addressed me
as light moving swiftly
from chair to table
to lie folded there like a white napkin

At last I broke the black silence
(was it I who spoke?)
The light stirred like some live thing
and fell on the wristbone of my right hand

That is how I know
it is you who came into the room

The light shimmers on my white wristbone
which throbs as if it were a pulse
It is you for whom it throbs
though my heart has stopped still

1967

Insomnia

After the bath
you lay on the bed
exposing layers
of beautiful washed skin
we both stared at in surprise;
long strands of hair, shiny and damp
under the yellow lamplight,
fell over your shoulders:
they made two exclamation marks
with your stiffened nipples.

And gently you fell asleep
at my side;
while I, my sweet, stayed awake
all night
who had your uncovered beauty
to think about,
your nipples troubling me
in the night
like two mysterious asterisks.

1967

On Seeing the Statue of Sappho
On the Quay of Mitylene

You look, Sappho,
like one of your own virgins
who has just been told
an off-colour joke
– such a simper

Not at all
as I imagine you
my loving, dark-skinned girl
with yellow hair
and a hand darting
into a man's tunic

No smarter are the citizens
of Mitylene today
than when you showed
yourself in the harbour
to sailors and merchants

Or to the soldier
whose cloak was dyed purple
and was Eros, you said,
on his way down
from heaven

Immortal poetess
you wrote of love
as it no longer is,
of desire without shame

I who have done the same
greet you with the sibylline words
you once sang.
'Dead, I won't be forgotten'
you can have no complaint

But I must go

Aphrodite
has taken care to have
a girl waiting for me
in Mithymna
with soft hands
and softer mouth

She's a sensible girl
and will not mind
if I say the first libation
is to you

Between our raptures
we shall think of you
this night

1969

The Way to Go

Envy, lust, my rare-scented queen,
    rule men's lives; lust declines
for time and use turn the love-muscle flabby
but envy takes a man right to the grave

Surviving, I note wryly, in the noblest
    it troubles me like wens
and deep pitmarks on the face of a woman
once loved for her beauty

I pray my last days on earth be mad
    with sexual desire
so that virgins scatter at my coming
like timorous pigeons and sparrows

And when I die, die my Love
    with a lascivious image
in my head: my hand slowly
ascending your hot uncovered thigh

1969

Hills and Hills

The hills
remind me
of you

Not because
they curve soft and warm
lovely and firm
under the Greek sun

Or flow
towards the horizon
in slow limpid waves
falling away mysteriously
at the edge of the sea

So that I can only surmise
their being there
beyond my gaze
and stare into the greyness

But because
a long time ago
you stared at them
as I am staring now

1969

Absence

Love,
I make a silence
out of your name
and dip
my hands into it

1971

A Strange Turn

A moment ago, in my embrace
She rode me like a Joan of Arc;
Then seeing my fifty-year-old face
Where Time's acids had burned deep their mark,
My head of hair coloured grey and rust,
And my old eyes wise with genial lust
She stiffened and held herself in check.

I felt her limbs slacken at my side
As sweetly she kissed my wrinkled neck;
Desire unspent had all but fled
Leaving behind its wraith, mere sentiment,
That poised her astride me motionless.
Ah, if my flesh were but firm, not loose,
And I were young, how she'd ride and ride!

1971

You and the Twentieth Century

On the one hand, dear girl, there's
this brutal stinking twentieth century;
on the other hand there is you
or rather your incredible sapphire eyes

Let me do some rapid mental arithmetic:
the big wars one and two, some smaller ones,
Auschwitz and Vorkuta, of course Hiroshima,
revolutions, massacres, executions and – Stalin

And as companion piece though lacking
the Georgian's consummate hypocrisy, Hitler;
such two you may be sure will never again be seen:
not even History can repeat her masterstrokes

Though once again the merciless pinheads are loose
in the streets, man-loving idealists are sniffing
human blood; the weak resenting their weakness
dividing neatly into demagogues and murderers

It's a familiar enough story, God knows
who uses the same old ploys to push us on
to meet the Messiah, i.e. death of course
who alone brings peace, redemption from lies and murder

I endure both what I know as memory
and as learning, as well as the day's outrages
hustling us inescapably into vulgarity and serfdom
because not otherwise can I know your beauty

Yet, love, when I see your incredibly lovely eyes
wise as an old woman's, bright with mischief,
it seems I can pick up the day as calmly as a child
picks up a forgotten toy from his littered floor

1971

Epitaph for a Poet

I sang of thighs
I sang of breasts
I sang of shoulders
soft and black as soot
white and soft as cloud
and of curved lips
from which kisses
fell like rose petals
or flew like birds
wilder and wilder
I sang
as I grew older
and my loins wrinkled
like the forehead of a sage

1971

Because my Calling Is Such

Because my calling is such
I lose myself whole days
In some foul cistern or ditch,
How should mere woman's love reach
Across the lampless silence
For the sake of that craze
Made blind Homer dance –

I, crouched in the rainless air
And choking with the dust?
Yet so bowed, the readier
To kiss your palm, my finger
Touching your fabulous face
Beyond all error and lust
In all that dark place.

For the trove of images
One gathers in the dark,
The dark that's piled with refuse
I shall not curse the bright phrase,
Coronal of my eclipse;
Though had you wed a clerk
He'd have your red lips.

Not driven like a lazar
From his house and children,
His embraces as he were
Frog on your white sheets, my dear,
Made mock of and rejected:
Who'd turn had you chosen
A prince on your bed.

1971

Talk at Twilight

Night
slides down
the smooth, immense
tooth
of day
like firemen
down a pole
and everywhere
stamps out
the garish light.

My love's voice
crackling
under my ear,
I smother it
in a blanket
of silence
soft
with tenderness
and irony.

1971

Memo to a Suicide

When I was mad
about her
I bought all her daubs
– money on the barrel:
she wouldn't have it
any other way –
took her to expensive restaurants
movies and plays
lit up her body
with flowers and jewels
and with the fever
of an aging lover
threw in a summer's idyll
on the Riviera

You, Luke, hanged yourself
so that she could see
your blue tongue
sticking out at her
when she found you

1973

Stella

All afternoon she sits in the doorway, a tourist attraction
    to be stared at by Greeks or the foreigners
Who know her story. Old and ill and her feet swollen
    to rhinoceros size,
Once, long ago, she was a wild creature so fair and disdainful
    she made the sober merchants dream at their tills
And fishermen haul in lascivious sea-nymphs all night long.
Their wives, even the comeliest of virgins, cursed her beauty
    praying their merciful God
To strike her with plague or leprosy. One day He lifted
    a petitioner's taper from its tiny brass socket
And turned it into a man handsome and clever with words,
    poet and talked-about novelist from another island.
She saw him and fell, his curious fire loosening her limbs;
In the crumbling Genoese castle, surrounded by ears,
    they made love.
The furious villagers rejoiced. At last the contemptuous beauty
    had been roiled in the mire
Her scented petticoats pulled over her head,
    her besmutted buttocks for all to see.
O the fetid dreams of men! How they besmeared the white
    breasts that had made them groan in their sleep.
How they reviled what for so long they had longed for in vain
While the women and girls so lit up the church
With grateful candles you'd think for weeks God's face
    was shining there.
He lifted yet another taper and blew out its flame: the teller
    of tales made off for Athens to compose
A moving novel about their tragic love and never saw her
    again.
But overnight she became the ruined unhappy heroine
    of a thousand lustful dreams
Such that aesthetes and bored rich women dream
And wandered from place to place to return at last

comfortless and impenitent
To her village and the filthy leers of men, the compassionate
     jeers of wives and virgins
To live solitary and infamous in the house where you see
     her now.
All that was long ago. Day by remorseless day
Her famed and troubling beauty crumbled into commemorative
     moles, wrinkles and yellowing parchment skin
And the heartbreak of an old woman's toothless grin.
Now there isn't a villager, old or young,
Who doesn't run up to embrace this hairy misshapen crone
     with the wild gone look in her eyes
And the sour excremental smell that fills up her doorway.
Not one who does not feel glad and right
Having someone whom daily he can forgive and pity
Or whose heart is not made proud to fix her hoary
     and humbled at the end of his benevolent stare;
Especially since the government itself is rumoured to allow her
     a small stipend to sit in the doorway
     to be gawked at, an Aeschylean lesson for all Greeks,
Her fabled loveliness caught forever in a work
     of imperishing art while her dying decrepit self,
A tourist attraction in the village, puts still more drachmas
     in the merchants' tills.

1973

Note: Rather than leave her village and enter a home for the aged in
Mitylene, Stella Ioannou ended her life by setting fire to herself, thus
dying as she had lived – a proud iconoclast and rebel. She is the heroine
of the well-known Greek novel, *The Schoolmistress with the Golden Eyes*,
by the distinguished novelist, Stratis Myrivilis. – I.L.

The Fine Excess

This the gods say binds love and genius:
The gift of extravagance, O boundless
Giving. They're like the prodigal sun
That without cease gives yet never grows less.

I know a mediocre sculptress
Who markets trinkets and saleable heads;
Diminished to this is woman's love
That turning regardful turns from excess.

Women I've loved and taken to bed
And they gave me all their nature allowed
But one woman gave without a thought
One woman loved greatly and she is dead.

1973

Inspiration

I have brought you to this Greek village
famed for its honey
as others are for their bread or wine
Love-making kept us awake
half the night
afterwards the jiggers took over
and would not let us sleep
Cocks and crowing women
woke us from our troubled doze
We compared laughingly the red bruises
on our arms and cheeks
Your good mouth, as it always does,
made me drool
and my spirit rose at once
In this stupid century
addlepated professors and mechanics
decry Inspiration
Alas, their arms have never held her;
gazing at you, woman,
in this shy early morning light I could more easily
doubt the feel of the bare boards under my feet
Truly this goddess has being
– in you, in some rare almost forgotten poems
and the mountainous hills and sea
which are waiting for us to look at them,
this vinestem curling on our windowsill
this bee
Come, let us show them
the fierce lumps on our divine foreheads

1973

Vampire

I'm not a dirty old man, my love
O I am not at all what men say I am;
For I am not wild over breasts and thighs,
Before the sweetest cleft my nerves are calm.

Be warned, my love, be warned and do not stay;
I'm a vampire who'll drain your youthful blood
For poems to feed his immortality,
Who'll give you horrid fangs and make you mad.

Young girls are what melt the ice in my veins;
Their sighs, loving glances are what I need.
When they awake my wanton lust for truth
Not rival Death himself can stay my greed.

And your daisy loveliness is your doom;
Run, my darling, run far away and hide
For I'm cursed to turn beauty into truth
And you, my sweet, into my spectral bride.

Ah, no, do not run but if you love me
End my accursed lineage and my lust;
If you would see them wither into dust,
Drive this stake through my heart and let me die.

1973

Young Couple at Lum Fong Hotel

Penang. December 7, 1973

When I see you
                    smiling
at each other
and nakedly showing
the appetite in your hands and eyes

I forget the chattering old men
                    with bladder trouble
and slack-bellied blear-eyed women
who moan
            over their hard nocturnal stools
as once with equal vehemence
they rocked and moaned
in the furious exertions of love

Each other's unbreaking pole
            of imagination and love
you vault over
            wisdom greying at the roots
and smelling of unalterable defeats,
the will-to-power that fleers
            out of skincreases and haemorrhoids

O my oblivious lovers
from my table
            I applaud silently
as you rise
with perfect grace and disdain

1974

I Think of Ovid

I think of Ovid and the merry twinkle
in his eyes as he fingerfucks the dressed-to-kill
matron sitting beside him while her husband
facing them on the opposite side of the table
feelingly decants on Plato's *Ion*
– he's no fool that man, knows a thing or two
about the arts, is even flattered by the famous poet's
attentions to his wife – and the other guests,
a noted critic of plays among them, a Proconsul
just returned from Alexandria and a clutch
of minor poets cutting their envious teeth
on Virgil's shanks but plainly intending Ovid's,
bare their teeth in vinous approbation. The husband
is very obviously pleased with himself
and the unexpected impression he's made on everyone.
His wife is beautiful, the much-sought-after Ovid
is sitting at her side, filling her glass
and paying her compliments that are making
her squirm and giggle with laughter.
It's a scene that would move anyone
always tuned-in like himself to what's significant
and meaningful in this wretched world
and always eager to seize whatever enjoyments
it keeps locked up in its hidden storeroom.
His educated mind calls the live composition
in front of him *Beauty and Fame* but swiftly
changes it round out of deference to Ovid's
greatness. He's touched to discover so much
sensibility in himself, such a quick and lively mind
– true, his host has not been stingy
with his best Falernian and the guests
have been attentive, even flattering
to the provincial pair though his good-looking wife
would win the heart of Caesar himself,

the old curmudgeon – and so he lets himself go,
pulls out all the stops and speaks with unwonted
persuasive eloquence and warmth, with real passion
about *poesis*, glancing at the renowned poet
from time to time to see how he's making out,
whether his words have been winged with divine fire.
Meanwhile Ovid all evening has been keeping up
a steady pressure on the proud matron's clit,
stroking it gently, using only one finger
– the experienced lecher – till he feels a gush
of cuntjuice, warm and viscous, suffuse
his finger and run down his wearied hand.
Only now does he smile to the moist-eyed husband
whom emotion has finally choked up. He smiles
approvingly, genially; he smiles from a full heart,
knowing that in an uncertain world
where death and a woman's scheming hypocrisy
are the only things a sensible man will bank on,
and men are black-hearted and joyless,
only the cold lusts of money and position
exciting them, the gods approve an innocent
fingerfuck giving pleasure to himself and the lady
and making her come – decorously as the occasion
required; and that this or the real thing itself
(screw the fine things promised by dictator or sage)
is a mortal good within our mortal means
before we join the joyless shades of Hell.

1974

September Woman

She unclasps her brassiere
and lets her breasts fall on his face
like ripe-heavy melons

He shuts his eyes
to imagine the many enraptured hands
that reached out for them,
the firm lips that once quivered with passion

He imagines her imagining him imagine this

The season's pathos envelops them
like an echo
and makes them one with the lonely stubbled field

However sweetly she smiles
he is aware of the silver fillings in her teeth,
the disappointed tenderness in her fingers
when she touches him,

Feeling on his bared skin
she is divided between desire
and the mockery of it
as she pushes her thick body under him

1974

Proteus and Nymph

I put down my book
    and stare at the distant haze;
the loud-voiced Greeks around me
    chomping on their fish and *peponi*
must reckon I'm having age-old thoughts
    on the human condition.
Noisy fools. I'm thinking of the waves
    gently cupping the breasts
of the lovely nymph just risen from the sea
    and the water lapping
her thighs and her delicate love-cleft

When she swims away
    she pulls my thoughts after her
in watery streaks of light. I become
    the sea around her
and she nestles in my long green arms
    or is held in the flowing
wavelets of my white hair. I billow
    above her like a dolphin
stroke her limbs and nip her rosy neck and shoulders
    with sharp unceasing kisses
till languorously she slips to the ribbed sand
    where under the haloing starfish
fern weed and enamoured seasnake I quiver
    between her silver thighs

1974

The Castle
Mithymna, Lesbos. July 18, 1974

They who built this castle
did they in its spacious courtyards dance
and did their fine ladies
display bejewelled hands?

Where are the fine ladies now
and where are their gallants?
All are gone, my love, all
grey dust under your heel

From this distant hill
the ruin looks like a trepanned skull
that mocks brides and fishermen
and even the stars and the sun

And you and all fine ladies
may see at any hour
the ironic scraping sand
dance in each crumbling tower

1974

To the Woman With the Speaking Eyes

It is not men you fear
but the tenderness they make you feel for them

And your resentment is not against men
but against the unfair division of the universe
into pestle and mortar, mountain peaks and valleys

Dark your beautiful eyes and tragic:
they have seen too many fearsome transformations
of smooth pluckable mushrooms into clubs and truncheons

Your desirable breasts are a burden to you
and though your Caesarean cicatrice
is an arrow that points directly
to where all men and angels would wish to lie
your supple pleasure-promising legs are closed
against them like inhospitable Abrahams

Unsure of the planets that rule, finally
you walk away hand-in-hand with your pride
leaving behind your modern confusion
for philosophers to unravel

1974

Reunion at the Hilton

You walked into my room
bringing the misspent years with you

Like two grey-haired children at play
we re-arranged them

First on your lap
then on mine

1974

Archilocos Versus Homer

For the sake of poetry I've done many vile things;
Slept with old hags, told pitiful lies to young ones.
Character and reputation lie both in ruins
But O my ponderous Homer, what poems, what poems!

1974

Farewell

She's gone. The one I swore up and down
to give a Greek villa and six children
if she married me, a trip around the world
to the moon, Mars, Venus
anywhere so that I could be with her
so great was the fire in my head,
in the sleeved arms that ached to hold her.

She's gone. The one that made me turn
restlessly from side to side each
sleepless night, thinking of her cool naked limbs
curled up on the lovestained sheets,
her red lips and long black lashes,
her smiles, her pouts, her sexy gestures,
the perfection of her small feet.

She's gone, whose laughter made me forget
the decorum of grey hairs,
children, friends, literary foes
the importance of being Trudeau, Pompidou, Spiro Agnew
or even the illustrious dust of Uncle Ho.
Let the whole world be damned, I said
and let the dead marry off the dead.

She's gone in whose arms I rose
resurrected after the third lay;
peace and wild joy and laughter were mine
for a while, but she's gone, gone in a bus
that with a snort has taken her far away
while the grey dust that settles over me
swirls and twirls like the ghost of an empty day.

1975

For my Distant Woman

I remember you as you were in Paxi,
my distant woman, and send my disconsolate thoughts
handspringing backwards like a clown eager for plaudits
to pick up your scents again, your smiles, your tenderness.

Agile and talented, he will never catch up with you
though to nudge him harder I've promised him top billing
in a floodlighted arena of his own choosing:
not even the cleverest dog could pick up your scent again.

My absent darling, fragrance and tenderness are strewn
on the silver ripples we both watched one night
when the full moon and all the stars were listening to us:
they cling to whispers beyond the reach of dog and clown.

Your blurring image enters my nostalgia softly
as the sun's semen enters the crimson flowercup
and often, as now, like the first heavy gout of rain
that makes it toss and shiver on its tender stem.

1976

Of the Man Who Sits in the Garden

You went away. For the last time
the hotel doors received and enfolded you
like a lover's arms. I was left standing
in the dark street like someone too dazed
by a car's sudden illumination to move,
imagining your ascension and the key
being turned to let you in, the blaze
you switched on revealing my empty place.
Did your lips tremble as mine did
when I turned down the silent street toward
the Byzantine church, our impeccable cue
to quicken step that we might ravenously
lock in an embrace and kiss hands, mouth, eyes
in the shadows a stone cherub had made for us?
When our lips touched did the cherub blow his trumpet?

On this island full of boats and trinkets,
of failed expatriates without love or joy
I remember another island and another day:
music, laughter, tenderness of eyes and hands,
the whitewashed square full of horny Greeks
made still hornier yet by your walking by,
your full uplifted breasts lifting their *peos*
till it seemed tables and backgammon boards
must topple unless their fine upstanding members did,
your quick stride luckily making the crisis pass
as swiftly as it arose with no boards smashed
or Greeks, young and ancient, cursing a ruined game.
More proud than the Sheba-escorting Solomon
or pint-sized Napoleon making it with Josephine,
I was Paris and you were my enchanted Helen.

In the purpling dusk I softly call your name
and quite bonkers think from behind that shuttered house,
or that stone, or the dark solitary cypress
that towers above the aerials standing perched
on the rooftops like an army of Martian birds
you must appear, so vast the longing in my arms,
the wild hungry hope in my staring eyes.
Soon the ballerina stars will come dancing out
as if on cue, and under the glittering diversion
they make the guerilla shadows linking massive hands
will darkly commandeer, my tremulous darling,
all your hiding places: cypress, stone, and house,
and push you into the garden where I sit writing this
and where each night under the speechless gaze of the moon
I bury my grizzled head between your naked thighs.

1976

For Francesca
Milano. November 28, 1974

Francesca
you have the name
of a woman
who should be my lover

I cannot sleep
and retell your name
over and over

The three syllables
make a music in my ear
no one has heard before

They ignite each other
into a flame
that lights my room's darkness
till I think the night has gone

The dawn comes
when I open wide my window
to let music and flame
astonish the whole world

1976

To Margaret

Aeons ago the African sun blackened your skin;
Africa looks through your eyes, walks on your elegant feet,
And Africa is in the suppleness of your limbs:
But the lope you serve me with – where is that from?

Let's see, your father was a Lowlander, your mother
Half Portuguese, half Kaffir black; and yet other
Strains are in you, did you say: French, German?
Truly an ingathering of nations under your own sweet skin!

Yes, sunk somewhere beneath your restless waves
Are the Dutch galleons, the Portuguese men-of-war;
And from time to time I can hear the tides pluck at them,
Turning them over stilly in their deep forgotten graves.

Luckily it's Africa predominates, shows through:
In your sureness, melancholy, ease and laughter.
You are a medley of many bloods, my dear mixed-up Margaret
But the puma that pads into my bedroom is wholly you.

1976

Discothèque
Hydra. July 3, 1975

Hey, I want a ringside seat
on that ass
with no one crowding me

It's an action poem
     a wrecker's ball
made wholly of air

That ass is pure magic
an invisible hypnotist
is swinging
    from side to side
to hook me
    on posterior analytics

I feel I'm going wall-eyed
into a trance

All I want to see
is that split-off dactyl
in cheeky faded blue-jeans
leaping out at me

It's a hopped-up pendulum
flicking out
    the frenzied seconds
for all of us

To that relentless thump
all the quaint escritoires
     of the past
are being carted off

~

& dumped into the waves below:
religion government philosophy art

On the floor of the discothèque
it's the tough heart-muscle
of the universe
               I see
pounding eternally away

1976

Seduction of and by a Civilized Frenchwoman

Having agreed that Simone de Beauvoir's feminism
is a bad joke
that Sartre is a has-been and a stupid
Jansenist muddlehead
that Camus possessed more integrity than talent
that there are no longer any poets in France
worth mentioning
that much the same could be said for her novelists
and that, in general, French culture
is in a parlous condition, if not actually dead
not having dared to move
a single centimetre beyond Flaubert and Valéry
and that no one except the two of us
seemed to know what is happening to that wretched country
having agreed politely to disagree
about Hemingway, Rimbaud, Hölderlin, Nietzsche, Brecht, Lawrence,
Moravia, Jaspers, Kafka, Strindberg, and Pasternak's *Dr. Zhivago*
having dismissed politics as a *bêtise* and religion as a *folie*

AND

Having inevitably but cautiously left the high ground
of literary and philosophical discussion
to speak of more personal, more mundane matters
i.e., one's dissatisfactions with conventional marriage, one's
adulteries, fornications, venereal diseases (there were none)
and given a description of the circumstances attendant on
        one's best and worst fucks
having slyly dropped two or three hints
about one's favourite erogenous zones and the best means
for stimulating them

~

and having led from this to the overriding, paramount need
     in sex for tenderness, mutual esteem,
humour, *délicatesse* and for similar though
not necessarily identical tastes in literature, music, philosophy,
art, theatre, and contemporary films
we are now ready to make love

1976

For my Incomparable Gypsy

The beauty that nature would fill
with pregnancies I'd keep sterile
forever, to be gazed at, not touched:
a poem, a canvas under glass.
What has the fine curve of your chin
the trim perfection of your thighs
to do with ripening and decay?
Your tongue-kiss drives all sense away;
touch: my member salutes the world.
By such old contraptions nature
infests our disgruntled planet
with newsprint-reading imbeciles
with costive runts scribbling verses
and ugly girls who make me ill.
The world is turning brassier
and brassier. Plain decency
has disappeared into limbo
or wherever it is virtues
no longer fashionable go;
madmen would abolish classes
and the law of gravitation
with one reckless stroke of the pen,
and the inflamed ignatzes cry
for muscleman or psychopath
to hive them in honeyed cages
where theirs is but to eat and die
and no throwback appear
to make them feel inferior.
From here on in it's all downhill,
downhill all the way. Fine manners,
love and poetry and what once
went by the name of form or style
— all have been rammed up a baboon's
red asshole. Or Hitler's. The world grows

~

each day safer for knaves and goons.
So my incomparable gypsy
I decline the invitation
your amazing body sends me,
though brain and instinct are programmed
to infecundate all beauty.
Go fuck and fill your womb with child,
in these lines you'll never grow old
but stay as fresh as the first kiss
you pressed on my impatient lips.
Marriages are for common clay;
for you I wish eternal day
not pukes and the rounded belly.
Only in this embalming poem
my unravished beauty be mine.

1976

Sylvia

Enchanting are the pale-blue eyes
like splinters of ice catching colour
from the containing wineglass and the excitement
she breathes out of her delicate candyfloss mouth,
her lips a blood-drop on whitest snow

At night she rides her moped
through streets her imagination has made for her
hammering at doors she closed just before
her arrival and astonishes herself
by having nobody answer her loud knock

Dressed in trailing chiffon she is bride
and priestess tumbling into courtyards
where only enchantment will raise the water
from rusted wells and scatter the necessary bits
to feed the brooding cats on the unmended sill

Elegant as crystal, quick-change artist
in her change of moods and clothes she patrols
like a trooper the fanciful and bizarre, imaging
for a shook-up world its unshakeable paradoxes
in the coarse longjohns worn under her evening silk

For the most fateful ride across the tracks
that divide her childhood from the fabled suburbs
she will subdue with an exquisite self-mocking look
she pulls her black hat down to her fragile nose
and adjusts the fatal feather boa around her neck

1977

Because You Squeezed Back

Because, O yes,
you squeezed back
and my hand became
liquid fire
in the crowded ascending elevator
melting gold
here we are in Paola
eating snappers
              basil-and-garlic spiced
our converse
with the three Italians
seated at the next table
billowing like light summer clouds
over heated fields
'buono' 'molto buono' 'bellissimo'

Not Leopardi, not Montale,
not even Fellini gifted and fat
could have written
a more surprising scenario

1977

The Puma

You are mistaken, he said
I am neither lecher nor womanizer.
If I'm crazy about women
it's for the beauty
some pitying devil threw over them,
a beauty that blinds my gaze to everything
except lips eyes breasts
and roils my blood
like a delicious venom.

When the fit is on me
I am their slave, their man Friday;
they can do with me as they will
and to their absurdest wish
I am as malleable as putty,
more pliant than straw.
For their ally is not beauty alone
but the scantness of sense or purpose
I find in the remotest curved niche
of the universe;
whoever framed its empty immensities
didn't reckon on a man's reason or conscience
or the unassuageable ache in my heart.

Women and poems are my sole chance here
to give expelled breath shape and contour
and fable it with meaning.
I place on the brow of every woman I love
a crown made from the choicest words;
I dress her like a woodland queen
in trope and metaphor.
My desperation blossoms into garlands
braceleting her wrists, my sick despair
into flowering anklets.

I plug the void with my phallus
and making love on bed or carpet
we transfigure pitchblack nothingness
into a tamed puma whose whiskers
we stroke between enrapturing kisses.

1977

Laurentia

Ste. Agathe des Monts. February 20, 1977

The loveliness of incorruptible snow
lying bunched on evergreens.
Am I mad that I see soft breasts everywhere?
I want to climb up to fondle and caress.

O the sensuousness of snow-covered hillocks:
a harem of naked women
inviting me to run wild among them and disport.

On all sides the winter displays
its voluptuousness made irresistible
by discipline and icy restraint.

But best I love the stillness
that coming down from the mountains
surrounds the grey trunks of trees.

When it releases me at the road's end
Laurentia will have a lover
fit to embrace her cold sensuality.

1977

Love Lament of a Mesomorph
Toronto. January 10, 1977

1:30. I brush the snowflakes off my collar.
I wait outside for her and shiver.
The world around me, all I can see of it
is white and cold. The street is strangely quiet.

Where is she, my beautiful Adrienne?
Ah, but she cares only for tall blue-eyed Englishmen.
I can stand here till Doomsday: freeze, sneeze, and cough.
What does she care for a poor unhappy mesomorph?

2:00. In this blizzard she will not come.
Go snowflakes, bring her this poem
and may it so inflame her, so dazzle
she'll think me blond, Anglo-Saxon, and six feet tall!

1977

Hidden Worlds

My young dog barks at the snowflakes:
white mice, they parachute down from the sky
in terrifying numbers, assault his fine head
and brown coat, drive him into the shed

Where he trembles out of cold and bewilderment.
His first November, his first snowfall.
My neighbour's house is sullen. Bitter.
the unbandaged shingles are streaks of stale blood

And each unlighted window stares back at me
with the suspiciousness of an old woman
though inside my head Artemis is dancing
and a god readies himself for his resurrection

A patch of snow. Greenery. On a ragged leaf
the season curls up and dies
as a surviving fly crawling on the windowpane
opens a road for us to oblivion

You are far away. On another continent.
A spider's filament connects our hidden worlds.
I think of you reading a poem, smiling
and suddenly the grass is white with white lilac petals

1977

Puppet Show With Dialogue

I must immortalize your breasts.

They sag.

Excellent. You shall possess
the only sagging breasts
poetry ever made immortal.

*When I look at them
my despairing thoughts fall down
farther than they.*

Nonsense. You must think of them
as humble resigned saints
kneeling for absolution.

*Your conceit uplifts
neither my breasts nor me.*

Well, then, your nipples:
they're two unopened rosebuds
dropped in the snow
to baffle an Alpine climber.
He plucks them from the snow
and starts an avalanche.

*Worse and worse.
What can you say about my cleavage?*

From the magnificent tower of your neck
it is a golden runway
for a flight into dark ecstasy.

Give me your hand, poet,
and let me fill your goblet
with wine.

I drink to you, O lovely lady,
and to your breasts
for they are the drooping eyelids
of a sleeping world dreaming
of perfection.

(The puppets, Poet and Woman,
clink glasses and embrace.)

1978

Lady on the Piazza

This morning I had spaghetti
al pomodoro with your wraith
after we'd greeted each other
at the Piazza di Spagna

It had your perfect mouth
your smiling melancholy eyes
and stroked my hand without cease:
smiles fell on me from the air

Who thought of thievish Romans
the violence in the streets
or in one's own soul?
Once more you worked your miracles

Only when I pressed against you
did you recede and disappear
and my aching fingers embraced
a vanishing waistline of air

Love, so long as I draw breath
this city is you, and I shall always see you
sitting on the steps of the piazza
surrounded by flowers and ruins

1978

David and Bathsheba

She gave herself to me and I was her god,
her king: nothing I did or could do
was ever mistaken or wrong. I was her Messiah
among men, tall and well-favoured and strong

As for my near-faultless psalms
in praise of the Lord and men of valour:
over their exulting strains she went simply mad
and would listen to them hour after hour

As God hears me, when I was frightened or sad
I was wise enough in the ways of woman
to keep far from her, aware compassion in women
puts to route all urgings of desire

Yet before the new moon was in the sky
she was mousing out my frailties, scanning my troubled soul
for lesions and cracks. I took my harp from the wall
and sang to sleep the froward slave and infidel

1978

The Chastening Years

A long time ago
I condemned the middle class,
loathing their crassness, their incurable philistinism

Then it was the prole,
seeing what a bent pin he is,
the ever-obliging tool for masters

Later I observed to friends
that though a few fevered souls
cared vehemently for freedom and uprightness
the many-too-many in all lands,
the superfluous ones,
think mainly about stuffing their craws

Now with the innocent guile
the chastening years bring
I have resolved to keep in mind
only your fabulous blue eyes and smile
and to live as though nothing else matters
but the delicate play of your hands

1978

Hummingbird

Myconos. June 14, 1977

Flaunting
their pirate's flag of pubic hair
in cool pairs
the firm-titted girls
go past me

Or they sprawl on the sand
giving their marvels to the sun

My turned head
is a hummingbird
sipping the dark flower
between their thighs

1978

The Tightrope Dancer

Awareness of death's pull
into nothingness
begets tyrant and sadist
but the prod, the harsh shove of love
makes the defiant artist
dance on his tightrope

1978

When Death Comes for You

When death
comes for you, my dear,
let him take you
like a candleflame
that is taken
from its wick
by a gentle stir
of wind
smelling of lilac

1978

Divorce

What is it about divorce
brings an estranged couple closer?
Here we are, Boschka, nearly twenty years later
reading our poems and stories to each other;
the fire blazes: its warmth is not greater
than what's in our souls;
we listen, comment, approve
and laugh like two grey-haired children.
Why now, not then, the love we display
exchanging news of friends and the universe
after a morning of rain and mist?
Arm-around-waist we walk, talk,
and always with the ease of those
who know their words and actions please.

Someone up there must be an ironist!
Or is it, seeing our soaped heads
in the mirror
who in hell wants to add more discord
to the general futility?
Let the dropped crabapple moulder where it falls,
the seed will clutch and break the soil.
Is that what love is: to care knowing
stars and blossoms flare to extinction?
We've separated wide the fingers of our hands
and let fall through them egotism, illusion, pride:
dear, dear Boschka, how tenderly now
our fingers entwine and hold.

1978

Poet and Woman

I can make poems only out of chaos,
out of hurt and pain.
I sing loudest when my throat is cut.

And saying this,
I handed her the razorblade
she lovingly slashed my throat with.

After, when she was sluicing the blood
into the enamelled urn
my sorrow was that I could not thank her.

Nevertheless out of that silence
my greatest poem was born: the one
she sings to the hairy Cyclops on her bed.

1978

Smoke

I've come to the tavern
to wipe away
with the back of my hand
your face, your caresses
and your perfume

How many glasses
will it take
before you become
as insubstantial
as the smoke from my cigar,
a grey chaotic turbulence
billowing into oblivion?

You are as unshakeable as death
you accompany me everywhere
like my own death
that is waiting for me
in a villa
or a Roman convent
where guarded by simple nuns
I shall write out
my theology of despair

When the memory of your hand
lingers on my shoulder or arm
when the recollection of your kiss
reddens my lips and cheeks
and the pupils of my eyes
distend with the curve
of your eyelashes
I begin to tremble

as if a shadow
had fallen across my grave

I am the stillness
I am the chewed cigar
I am the emptied glass
I am the scattered ash on the floor
and I am the grey smoke
that wreathes your beloved image
forever and forever
though it drifts and dissolves
in the white morning sunlight
that comes from the doorway
to falter on table and bar

1978

Fata Morgana

Perhaps tomorrow but not today, not now,
I'll smile at the grotesque picture I have
of myself sitting on your broadloomed floor
and reading poems to you, setting off
a jubilee of flambeaus and girandoles,
of conceits and happy valley fantasies
with a lover's fond rant Byron's hero
might have envied in his Venetian prime.

For you're as mad as they come, my dear,
and had not itch or vanity bewitched me
and the astonishing beauty of your face
I'd have read accurately the telltale signs
on your mouth, the blankness of your blue eyes
when you suddenly fell silent and only
your uneasiness and paranoia
rushed in to fill their sad vacancies.

At that moment I was an idiot babbling
to an imbecile, a ludicrous old fool
entertaining with trope and metaphor
a sick Aphrodite sighing on her sofa
whose only signal that she still lived
was a muffled cry of pain and horror
like someone startled into strangled speech
by her own foul dreams and apprehensions

May my rabbinical ancestors forgive me
but I groan aloud and grow pale remembering
how I gently put your hand in mine, saying:
'I'll work hard to be worthy of your love.'
Lofty declaration to a moping screwball!
O the folly a poet will say or do
when a woman's beauty ravels his senses.
O the squalid comedy of his blinding love.

But you are the world each poet courts,
prodigally expending his ardour and wit
on her service, transfiguring her dullness
and forever reading immense subtleties
into her vacant depthless stares,
the slow lunatic smile on her lovely lips.
So pardon's the word, my sweet bedlamite,
and may all your dreaming be of peace and joy.

1978

For Sandra

Frenzied in my rented room
as I live and scarcely breathe
   I can think of nothing
but your blue fabulous eyes
your rounded full breasts
   and the fragrance of your hair
each time you moved or turned your head;
the delicious parts you let me kiss
and those you covered with a dazzling smile.

It is 4 A.M.
and sleep is far from my tired eyes
   I am an insomniac
with a pen in my hand
a lunatic praising your beauty
   over and over again
to the framed darkness outside
and the frantic insects
scrabbling on the window-screen.

Did you, O lovely lady,
really unhook the interposing bra
   and taking my hand
to your alerted nipple
did you, holding it there, really whisper
   after a long surrendering kiss
'I did that for my own joy, Love, not yours'
– or have I fallen asleep at last?
and am I dreaming this?

1978

Snake Goddess

for Heidi Montreal. October 1, 1978

I was here. I did these things.
I was a snakewoman. I danced to Indian chants.
I swallowed fire. Look at this picture of me,
proud dark-haired woman dancing flamenco.
I was everywhere. New York, Scranton, Miami.
In Boston they called me Chez Heidi: then
I was more supple than the rattler
I wound amorously around my neck.
Bitten on arm or thigh I ended up four times
in the hospital to notices that swelled
the ever-hopeful crowds and made me weep
for my wicked ten-foot babe that couldn't read.
Lying on the white sheets I ate them up,
caressing my limbs firm and beautiful
under their coverlet. I was an artist, mister,
never a boob girl in a cheap bar
swinging tassels from her tits,
though one night when I did a take-off on her,
making my buttocks twirl the silk cords
in silver circles, the whole place exploded
with applause. Ah, nights each gesture of mine
of hand or foot was instinct with life
and the fire I swallowed was less bright
than that which blazed inside me. Look at this photo,
and this one, and now this one. Here,
were it not for the dress I wear, you'd say
I am the flame lapping my own body
with its myriad snake-tongues
before I melt into each man's pocket
and scorch his living groin.

1979

Letter to A Lost Love

We can speak the words, my dear, of forgiveness
but only our actions could have healed us;
now we're both doomed to incompleteness
and to grimace as though with Bell's palsy.
I was just beginning to see through words,
my friend the enemy, the tricks he plays
with false bottoms and sawed-up ladies,
the will-o'-the-wisps he'd have me take for real;
you, at last, to see me with love's insight,
the compassion that only wisdom gives.
Now we're like the absurd figures of Pompei
forever arrested in a vague stance,
a gesture never to be completed,
dumb in the stillness our lava's made.
How words have fooled me all these years,
deceived me like the witches on the heath:
yet poor Macbeth was a poet also
and only poets can misconstrue where
the Banquos without a stitch of imagination
see only hideous misshapen hags about
and rightly smell the mess they're cooking.
If a Banquo croaks it's only because
an assassin's prosaic poniard
gets him in the gut; it's never dreams,
or ambition, the mad reaching out for greatness
and distinction, an immortal name
defying old Skull-and-Bones bringing
oblivion in his grinding white molars.
So farewell, my love, a long, long farewell;
maybe the Atlantic will wipe out the guilt,
the knowledge of wrongs done and suffered;
maybe in some other life I'll be asked
to cover the fourth wall of Paradise
and unlike del Sarto not have to choose

betwixt love and art but, blessed, have both.
But in the here and now I have a misery
to last my life and if I don't tear a hole
in my heart as wide and deep as its pain
it's because I've Byron's way of seeing things
and think death even more absurd than life
and once dead there's no more laughing then.

1979

For Harriet

I am a matchflare
you are another
      Together
for an instant
we pierce the surrounding
dark

Two matchspurts
I'd have us be
      Not wicks
that flicker
to extinction
and black silence

I love all passing things:
roses and dust
      Their brief stay,
like your smile, instructs me
to embrace the world
with irony and joy

1979

The Final Coming

Her lips were round and full
And to his lap she bent;
He saw no car ahead
And when he came he went.

1980

For Edda

In your kitchen
you enacted for me
neither Clytemnestra nor Lady Macbeth

But with no make-up,
with merely a single look, a single touch,
you gave your finest performance:
that of a woman of wit, charm, and liveliness

In that vast invisible amphitheatre
where sit the severest critics,
the enraptured shades of departed lovers
applauded you with my silent hands

1980

The Annunciation
Niagara-on-the-Lake. June 4, 1980

What angels will we meet on the way to the post office?
What kisses will the leaves rain down on your neck?
Your footsteps leave no shadows on the ground
for the morning sun makes a bale of them
which he tosses over the first white fence that we pass

The announcing angel robes himself in ordinary dress.
What name does he whisper in your perfumed
and delicate ear? Judith? Deborah? Eve?
When you incline your fragrant head to listen,
the storewindows blaze and shine and the village street

Robed in its summer foliage resounds like a West Point
salute with the sound of uncorked champagne bottles;
all the birds in the street take the happy noise
for cues and suddenly whole orchestras of them
and the singing choirs of girls and boys

Make such a jubilation, it frightens off
all evils and sorrows forever; your burgeoning form
parts the air before us like a sorcerer's wand
and the angel in ordinary dress extricates a wing
and blesses its bounty with his own bright feathers

1981

Vikki

You bring me news
of someone
I loved a long time ago
– you, her daughter.

Achingly I retrace your lineaments
into the large brown pools
and flame-red cheeks
that once made a fool of me.

If you wipe away five decades
I was an urban pod
bursting with poems and *vivas;*
I was young and crazy with love.

Your mother's love
was socialism and Lenin;
she once sobbed for hours
when I called him mad and vicious.

That mean-souled Tartar
took away her youthful bloom,
her husband, her handsome dark-eyed brother:
the first shot, the other driven to suicide.

In a Stalinist camp
his minions even finished off your grandmother:
fiery, sharp-tongued Bolshevik,
a cigarette forever dangling from her lip.

In your own quivering mouth
and uncertain stare
I read contemporary history
and graph my love's lost hopes and illusions.

1981

Ashtoreth

Yesterday you leaked headaches
on the sofa. Your face was white with pain
and when I took your cold hands in mine
they were colder than cold stone.

From kissings and love play to this:
a venter that Time inflates like a child's balloon;
an unSartrean nausea – the real thing –
over chicken wings you used to devour.

At night you stare at a moon
sans flags and footsteps and still a goddess.
Does she know something you don't?
Would you like to feel her belly?

How many wombs have grown big under her gaze?
How many navels have expanded in Lapland alone?
In Peking and Madrid? O tellurian bubbles
that swell and swell and after nine months pop!

And every night comes the same young raccoon
to attack our garbage pails.
I think you know the creature's hunger and madness.
Her fears. Life's so precarious.

You sigh and tremble in dark corners.
And quite suddenly you'll become silent
and all my love and questionings
bounce off you as though you wore a radar screen.

You make your own queendom wherever you go.
You carry life inside you, precarious and precious.
You give me your mouth to kiss
and your face lights up the whole room.

1981

Portrait of a Modern Woman

For her, sex is something she holds in reserve;
alienated from her real inner self,
it's tended with care like some exotic plant
to allure the stray butterfly to her sill.
She takes yoga classes and watches what she eats,
is prudent about money and emotions
but unfurls her independence like a flag.
Having been in analysis for insight
(so she informs me) and not therapy
she discusses love as an abstract painting,
a flowing involuted figure by Moore.
She likes catching it out when it makes its spring
and holding its quivering form up to the light,
yet wonders why it blackens and disappears
or grows into some bloated attachment
that mocks her with mouths shaped like grotesque suckers.
An artist in living, she swears by passion
and spontaneity, mistaking fervent
loquacity for something she's too cool,
too cautious to possess, too ungiving
in the modern sense; dismaying the lost men
who circle around her long shapely neck
until they break from the enchantment and run.
It always baffles her she's so much alone
or with old lovers, mostly now with women,
for her mirroring image shows her beautiful
and the great Moore had once praised her talent.

It would be a mercy to make her see
the fault's not entirely hers; it's in the stars,
in the revolving potter's wheel that's sent the sexes
flying off in contrary directions to wander
among sapless words that hang in the air
like stricken November leaves no wind has come
to shake loose. Dry November leaves, my dear,
whose ghostly rattle when a small breeze stirs them
expresses your sad vacancies for the world.

1982

The Breast Stroke

May the gods be praised that I should meet
on my final lap to the eternal sea
one so young, so gracious and lovely,
under clear skies promising as herself.
Ankled deep in the scorching sands
I can hear the shouting tide; in it
invitation and menace like the smile
on the fair face of my companion,
making me wish to nuzzle forever
between her firm thighs and cover
her mouth with long hungering kisses.

Insensate to everything but her warm flesh
I'd float out into the voluptuous sea,
my practised breast stroke perfect at last.
The heaving mounds press against me,
alluring me past the white wavecrests
that close behind like tall portals
barring return. Green towers collapse
on bright medallions larger than suns;
the virginal foam breaks into bridal cries
and after the last loud crash of savaging breasts,
into the long silence that no man hears.

1982

Blind Man's Bluff

The long dark September nights are come,
reminding the vacant poet of losses;
there are no stars in his skull,
only blackness, the fumes of dead loves.

Jerusalem is ruined and pillaged
and her kings and queens are grimacing marionettes.
Where is majesty? Beauty? The courtesies of love?
The stiffening valour in sinew and thigh?

They lie unnoticed on his kitchen floor:
broken pieces of wood, the colours dissolving
into echoes a rising wind amplifies
to a pitch his wearied heart no longer hears.

After each night's solitary meal
he plays blind man's bluff with shadows
that recite lines from his own poems
to mock him as he reaches out hands to touch.

Old poets know that game well.
Designs of soft vulvas cover the walls. Only when
he removes the tight blindfold from his eyes
will a fleshless mouth kiss him with his own passion.

1983

The Divine Touch

I was dejected from an old love
when she came to me
with her warm young limbs.
It was an unexpected gift from the gods
who have for their service
the happiness of grey-haired poets;
knowing in their untroubled pavilions
that the ripest wisdom falls
only at the touch of firm breasts
and long rippling thighs.

1983

Jude the Obscure

Yesterday I pulled my bobsled
up the highest hill
in our slum neighbourhood

Slow and thick the snowflakes
fell on my head.
I became the wonderworld around me.

I do not remember ever
turning the bobsled around.
What am I doing in that woman's bed?

1983

Of Leaves and Loves

Once a seed, now a tree crowned with leaves
that soil and sun, a *principium* of individuation,
shaped to hang for a summer and then fall.

Stars moulder and rot at a slower rate
or blaze suddenly into blackness
only to bud again on God's unfolding arm.

So my love was a quick seed
whose soil was your smile, its sun your joy.
A sudden frost turned its leaves black.

Black as the black night at my window.
No star will return to pierce the darkness.
No leaf ever bud on my withering stalk.

1983

The Hairy Monster

His old fingers making wet
the hairy monster under her lace tunic,
he hears the deft-handed goddess
tell across the torn coverlet
how once, still a copper-haired *kori*
in Piraeus,
she watched her grandfather
slit the pig's throat
ear to ear;
afterwards hearing
the hot blood of the crazed animal,
dying on his four trotters,
spurt into the white enamel pot;
all the while thinking
of the small fast thunders
the first gouts of rain
made on her roof,
the wind howling all night long:
a decrepit satyr lost
briar-trapped in the dark, dank grove
and in pain.

1983

Odd Obsession

I've seen your singular smile elsewhere.
On sun-warmed Mediterranean statues
of the late Alexandrian period.

With your fragile, ever-smiling lips you appear
both sensual and ascetic, a coin's toss
sending you either way.

The curves of your mouth bracket your secret.
Which are you? Mary, mother of Jesus,
or that other Mary, the scarlet Magdalene.

Your secret is that you don't know.
So you smile often to conceal your confusion,
giving you that strange look that intrigues us all.

Your lips obsess me like a misremembered word.
I can't remove them from my head, or imagine
any greater triumph than to blot them out forever.

At fourteen I made an older girl
articulate 'prunes' over and over again
because her mouth shaped beautifully pronouncing it.

Yours, I finally conclude, is the smile of a woman
who, figure and face making her irresistible,
mocks her lovers' immoderate passion.

But mostly mocks the world and herself,
knowing how brief are the days of beauty;
how cruel and fleeting the loves they inspire.

1983

New Year's Poem for Veneranda

When she climbs the steps of her basement apartment
she leaves the place in absolute darkness
except for the small mirror in my mind
that holds her surprised reflection.

I polish it till her confident smile
lights up my eyes and when I whisper
in the dark: 'I love you with all my heart,'
the corners of the room begin to shine.

She will bring wine and two goblets
and we'll toast my familiar daimons,
my obsession with her mad-making limbs:
cry window-breaking huzzas for her vagrant soul.

I've flicked off the years, one by one:
'This one loved me, this one didn't.'
Tonight I'll give her the denuded stalk
and it will turn a sunflower in her hand.

1983

Bonded

With you gone
I embrace pain,
pleasure's indisseverable twin

I would not unpartner them
even if I could

And I can't
        with you gone
and I, in our bed,
alone

1983

Rendezvous at the Coffee Mill

Will you be as beautiful
　　　as I imagine you?
As sensitive and tender?
　　　Unloyal or true?
Will you have a sense of wonder
or will you be a pious clod
　　　imploring an ignorant god?

Few women delight for long.
　　　Most disappoint.
A sly malcontent
　　　lies wound up in each.
As I hope to live
a thousand years for my sins
　　　their poor souls are costive.

When I was young
　　　I adored every girl
that stopped my breath.
　　　I lived only for their smiles.
But hopes run with the years
and love brings to this life
　　　dissension and strife.

At this hour, only a name,
        still unseen, unknown,
time is weaving you
        on this loom of possibility.
When you emerge at 9 P.M.
fully shaped from his frame
        how will you greet me?

Who will you be?

1983

Medusa

Her hair painted henna red
blazed suddenly into fire
and he fell back before her face,
his mouth dry with horror.
Mean-eyed carrion birds
flew from her twisted lips
and the leaping streaks on her head
coiling and uncoiling like snakes
chilled the blood in his veins.
Transfixed by dread
he was freezing into stone
when he remembered how often
her mouth had given him
   the gift of tongue,
how often her beautiful mouth
had praised his poems.

Out of Pure Lust

The tight sweater she was wearing
showed off her good points at once;
luckily she had an attractive mouth
that lifted my thoughts so that my mind
raced to it from her twin attractions,
settling on neither long enough
to put a glaze on my devouring eyes.

At twenty-one she was explaining for me
why nobody wrote love poems anymore.
'Love's unsatisfied lust, nothing more.
If I want a man I jump into bed with him.
Who needs his heated fantasies, or mine?
I've learned a thing or two about poets:
the only sheets they soil are those they write on.

'If a lover has been fondling my breasts
why should he wish to dream about them
or cudgel his brains to put my nipples into a poem
when he can pop them into his mouth
like ripe berries? I prefer it, mister, that way.
So does he, I'm sure, my breasts are so round and firm.'
She stopped and I wondered what old Petrarch would say.

Or lecherous Alighieri who made his Beatrice
immortal by putting his lust into an inferno.
What if she and Petrarch's Laura had been a good lay
and spoke of their lovers as they might of artichokes,
of ecstasies and fiascos, one-night stands,
finding the comedy of sex too funny for words?
What masterpieces would each have ripped off then?

1983

More Champagne, Darling
for Patrick Crean

Odd, that like myself you've been married
four times;
and yet I could have foretold your story
at our first greeting.

You're much too good-looking for clamorous women
to leave alone
and your subtle intelligence is no defence
against their resolution.

Your vanity needs their nurturing attention
and flattery;
too soon you discovered the immense world of commonness:
their loves singled you out.

You have the hedonist's scorn for strife and busyness,
the moiling masses;
believing a sensible man will find all of life's charms
in a champagne glass.

Anyway, that it's a fine talisman against the emptiness
that comes as much with success
these days as with failure, leaving you ever-hungering
for a woman's kisses.

At the end what's the litany? Betrayals:
loves, hopes for the human race,
the traitorous face, the incontinent bladder.
The press of flesh on flesh staves off surrender.

For we're romantics, you and I; in our century near kin
to the sick Christian
in a Christless world whose bleak terrors we choose to inter
between a woman's thighs.

1983

Central Heating

The dog runs past,
taking my thoughts of Infinity with him;
at the corner
he's swallowed up in it
and when he clambers back
I observe he has three heads
and his coat is scorched.

Not one of the nobs
will tell me where it's been
or what Greek it encountered
or the name of its dentist.
I light my cigar
at their singular redhot tail.

It's pointless to explore
the subject of Love with them
or Beauty or Man's Fate
on this planet.
Philosophy and Art
only make them growl;
in their collective minds
everything is cut and dried
and fixed forever
and there is only Hell.

But why does my head spin
at the sight of a beautiful woman
and the swirl of her skirt
pleasure me with hurt?
And why am I,
who find a leaf mysterious
and a spear of grass
or the bark of a dog
or croak of a frog
confident as if I'd been told
that not Hell, O not Hell,
but Love alone provides
the central heating for the world?

1983

Aristocrats
Naples. April 15, 1982

Beautiful, wearing a silver crucifix,
Rosa works in the waterfront bar
as a call girl who does not answer.

All the girls jump from their stools
when the Neapolitans point at them
– but not Rosa.

When the young mafioso
orders her up to bring his rum and Coke
she offers him the tribute of a slow smile
and takes her time.

Sensing he's different from the others
and knows his worth,
knows he has the sharpest knife
in the city
and two Alsatians that love him.

1983

Veneranda Dancing

She dances like a solitary Bacchante

The tight mini-skirt she flicks
before my eyes
is a leopard's ever-changing
spots

On the crowded dancefloor
she dances like someone possessed
and I am lost to all
except the motion
of her disordering limbs

When she dances like that
I can follow her down
all the way down
into the smoky bowels of hell

1983

Lady Macbeth

Once every month she becomes Lady Macbeth.
Then watch out! The glass she holds up to the light
for greasespots, the dishes fringed by soapsuds,
could be the last his eyes might ever see.
Knives are not the only things that kill.
He can be knocked cold by a flying coffee-pot
if there's enough force or venom in the throw.
Right now he means less to her than a stranger.
If she were an Arab and he an Israeli soldier
she could not hate him more or be more hostile.

Okay, he thinks, now she's a bloody communist
with a red flag between her legs. Should he stand up
and sing the Internationale? In a foul state
from unacted murders, her feelings of guilt
only make her more wretched and explosive. He strains
to remember her enormous capacity for love
and self-surrender, her gentle nature. At mealtimes
he distracts with sophistries that would do
a seminarian proud. The proverbial eggshells
can be heard cracking when she's hovering close.

His forbears were smarter. The crazy woman
was told not to show her strained face
until sanity returned. That way, tempers remain
unfrayed; and love, Thanatos' most exotic flower,
blooms in the mild air, its petals unscorched
by egotism and vanity, their own dust
over which now spread love's fragrance and delight
giving their chemicals to its sweet unfolding.
Patiently he must wait for the child's flood of tears
to wash the week's defilement from their shaken souls.

1984

Epistle to Catullus

You, Cat, fell for a patrician whore
who scoured the alleyways after dark
    looking for an Ethiop's
        hanging ballocks;
fascinatingly evil she was, also witty,
for when told to her face
        she loved cock dearly
she burst out laughing:
'You've said a mouthful.'

Still, compared to that broad
your uncle's saddled himself with
      in Verona
Lesbia's a vestal virgin.
Listen, that jerk your uncle
has got himself a real lulu
      this time:
one eye is without sight
and every morning she startles him awake
with trumpetings
Caesar's legions might envy,
      so dismal is her stomach.
and her teeth – it's the truth, man –
are dissolving in her mouth
      like long icicles,
simply wearing away from her gums
like the shoreline in Calabria.

That's not the end of it, Cat.
Piles ring the darling's asshole
    like a mare's halter
and a flaming herpes
    makes penetration
a risky business.

1984

Boschka Layton 1921-1984
Santa Rosa. February 17, 1984

Because each act of creation is a miracle
that happens again and again
until it becomes familiar as an autumn leaf
or a ripening appletree in full sail

I shall remember you not as charred bone and ash
to be given to earth's mad alchemy
but as the full-bosomed woman whose lips
mouthed my awed whisper: 'We shall make handsome children'

Your heart's vital joy apparent in the eyes of friends,
in children's smiles and the smiles of old women,
it is presumptuous to speak now of your crazy defiance
idle to praise the harsh devotions of your life

Ordinary miracles to pry open the eyes of the blind
happen every day. And my deep faith holds:
sun, wind, rain, and the dark nights will change
my Boschka's cinders to deathless apples and poems

1984

The Investiture
Paros. May 27, 1985

You bend to remove the beachpebble
from your sandal;
and as you straighten to greet me,
your smile, showing your strong white teeth,
reminds me I trod these shores once before.

With a woman who devoured me
as if I were a marine delicacy
snared from its tranquil cove; who,
another Eve, let me discover
evil and creativity are twinned,
are one.
        The hills and brackish years between
keep her image in a separate frame.

The same barren hills and widening sea;
the same rumpled many-colour'd Joseph's coat,
the same, yet not the same.

For now, my face a warrior's Achaean mask,
it is I who invest these hills, this sea,
with their boundless calm.

1986

Carmen
Montreal. July 12, 1985

Passion is lawless, always off-limits.
Formless. For Carmen with breasts like bull's horns
is forever in a rut. A voracious slut,
she wants her quickie here and now
on cloakroom floor or bed smelling of man-sweat
and lotion. Enter her opposite number
with fore-ordained knife sharpening in his brain.

Antonio's clip is murderous at the end;
for fearful the republican years
must cripple fine legs and shoulderblades,
he rages against the lean competing rivals, the fire
that still blazes in their rubbed-down loins
and with a final lunge translates insolent lust
into the chill perfection of death.

Until that fair moment let Carmen
prance and dance.

1986

Black Tourist in Tinos

Her motions are off-key;
the unused limbs quiver.
It's apparent she does not know
the steps to the Greek dance.
But her wild eyes close in a trance
and every black inch
of her festive body
is alive with kefi.

When she seizes the hem
of her dress, showing pocked thighs,
the island gods are happy.
So is every mortal
in the *kafenion,*
for her tremulous flesh is on fire,
and the flame licks her
till she melts like wax.

Her clumsy, joyous dancing
burns away chains and gyves,
makes of form itself a ruinous blaze.
The fire, only the fire matters,
the impulse in awakening seed.
When she leaves, taking her dark skin,
the lit place loses radiance
and we become patient mortals again.

1986

Diverse Pleasures

So my neighbour, a Greek virgin of fifty,
takes it all out on her poor canine
who's much too dumb to know why she calls him
'she' and washes his underbelly every chance she gets.

Living alone in her many-roomed house,
she troubles my mind, mostly when the dog
barks and barks as if in pain or fearful
of the devil alone knows what. At night

Before I fall to sleep, I hear him whimpering
outside the shut door, bewildered that stroking hands
can roughly seize and fling him on stone steps
and not turn again to fondle, or squeeze his toes.

Each Sunday she greets me on her way to church,
her eyes' happy gleam always making me think
of a sadist who sights for the first time
the white buttocks readied for his stinging rod.

In the afternoon, fat and aproned,
she tends her roses and hyacinths, trims her hedge.
The wornout dog sleeps under the porch.
A light rain washes the roadside dust from the leaves.

1986

Tristezza
for F. Ruberti

He showed me his painting of the Po,
canvas after canvas after canvas
until I thought he was out
to drown me in his studio.
Then he switched to nudes. Again it was
canvas after canvas but now they were
all of the same young woman whose hair
he coloured differently, each time
doing some altering thing
to her neck or mouth. He'd painted her
earthy and withdrawn, sensual,
a far-away look in her grey eyes.
Yet what I remember are not the soft
pastel shades, the disciplined tints
in river and woman, or how I kept thinking
the river could be the woman's unshed tears.
No, what stays in my mind is the silence
that filled the cluttered room
after he had finished speaking
and the terrible sadness for which
there are no words, no colours anywhere.

1987

I Take My Anna Everywhere

I take my Anna everywhere.
She is so beautiful she can break
a man's heart with a look,
the proud thrust of her shoulder.

She tells me she will die young.
I tell her all beautiful women have the same
premonition. Brevity is the stamp
of beauty, sealing it in the mouths of men.

I take my Anna everywhere.
She has the unpitying gaze of a goddess.
All the men who see her
want to live their wrecked lives forever.

A Note on the Text ∾

This selection was originally edited by Russell Brown with
Irving Layton. Additions to this new volume have been selected
by John Metcalf.

The poems, dated by first book publication, originally appeared in
*Love the Conqueror Worm, In the Midst of My Fever, The Long
Pea-Shooter, The Blue Propeller, The Cold Green Element, Music on a
Kazoo, The Bull Calf and Other Poems, The Improved Binoculars,
A Laughter in the Mind, A Red Carpet for the Sun, The Swinging
Flesh, Balls for a One-Armed Juggler, The Laughing Rooster, Collected
Poems* (1965), *Periods of the Moon, The Shattered Plinths, Selected
Poems* (1969), *The Whole Bloody Bird, Nail Polish, The Collected
Poems of Irving Layton* (1971), *Lovers and Lesser Men, Seventy-Five
Greek Poems, The Pole-Vaulter, For My Brother Jesus, The Covenant,
The Love Poems of Irving Layton, Droppings from Heaven, For My
Neighbours in Hell, Europe and Other Bad News, A Wild Peculiar
Joy, The Gucci Bag, Dance with Desire, Final Reckoning* and also in
the portfolio *Shadows on the Ground*.

Contents ⌒

Index to First Lines 〜

Also by Irving Layton ⌒

Here and Now 1945, *Now Is the Place* 1948, *The Black Huntsmen* 1951, *Cerberus* (with Louis Dudek & Raymond Souster) 1952, *Love the Conqueror Worm* 1953, *In the Midst of My Fever* 1954, *The Long Pea-Shooter* 1954, *The Blue Propeller* 1955, *The Cold Green Element* 1955, *Music on a Kazoo* 1956, *The Bull Calf and Other Poems* 1956, *The Improved Binoculars* 1956, *A Laughter in the Mind* 1958, *A Red Carpet for the Sun* 1959, *The Swinging Flesh* (Poems and Stories) 1961, *Balls for a One-Armed Juggler* 1963, *The Laughing Rooster* 1964, *Collected Poems* 1965, *Periods of the Moon* 1967, *The Shattered Plinths* 1968, *Selected Poems* 1969, *The Whole Bloody Bird* 1969, *Nail Polish* 1971, *The Collected Poems of Irving Layton* 1971, *Engagements: The Prose of Irving Layton* 1972, *Lovers and Lesser Men* 1973, *Seventy-Five Greek Poems* 1974, *The Pole-Vaulter* 1974, *The Darkening Fire* 1975, *The Unwavering Eye* 1975, *For My Brother Jesus* 1976, *Taking Sides* (Prose) 1977, *The Covenant* 1977, *The Poems of Irving Layton* 1977, *The Uncollected Poems of Irving Layton* 1977, *The Tightrope Dancer* 1978, *Droppings from Heaven* 1979, *An Unlikely Affair* (Letters) 1980, *From My Neighbours in Hell* 1980, *The Love Poems of Irving Layton* 1980, *Europe and Other Bad News* 1981, *A Wild Peculiar Joy* 1982, *The Gucci Bag* 1983, *Waiting for the Messiah* (Prose) 1985, *Korean Selection* 1985, *Fifty Greek Poems* 1985, *Swedish Selection* 1985, *Love Poems: New Edition* 1986, *Dance with Desire* 1986, *Final Reckoning* 1987, *Fortunate Exile* 1987, *A Wild Peculiar Joy: Selected Poems 1945-89* 1989, *A Wild Peculiar Joy: Selected Poems 1945-89* (audio) 1990, and *Fornalutx: Selected Poems 1928-1990* is forthcoming.

Volumes edited by Irving Layton include *Canadian Poems 1850-1952* (with Louis Dudek) 1952, and *Love Where the Nights Are Long* (with illustrations by Harold Town) 1962.